THE OFFICIAL
POLDARK
COLORING BOOK

The Poldark novels by Winston Graham

Ross Poldark • ***Demelza*** • ***Jeremy Poldark*** •
Warleggan • *The Black Moon* • *The Four Swans* •
The Angry Tide • *The Stranger from the Sea* •
The Miller's Dance • *The Loving Cup* •
The Twisted Sword • *Bella Poldark*

Also by Winston Graham

Night Journey • *The Merciless Ladies* •
The Forgotten Story • *Take My Life* • *Cordelia* •
Night Without Stars • *Fortune Is a Woman* •
The Little Walls • *The Sleeping Partner* • *Greek Fire* •
The Tumbled House • *Marnie* • *The Grove of Eagles* •
After the Act • *The Walking Stick* • *Angell, Pearl and Little God* •
The Japanese Girl (short stories) • *Woman in the Mirror* •
The Green Flash • *Cameo* • *Stephanie* •
Tremor • *The Ugly Sister*

The Spanish Armada • *Poldark's Cornwall* •
Memoirs of a Private Man

THE OFFICIAL
POLDARK
COLORING BOOK

**A COLORING ADVENTURE
IN CORNWALL**

*ILLUSTRATED BY
GWEN BURNS*

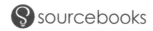 sourcebooks

Published by Sourcebooks, Inc.
P.O. Box 4410, Naperville, Illinois 60567-4410
(630) 961-3900
Fax: (630) 961-2168
www.sourcebooks.com

Originally published as *The Poldark Colouring Book* in 2016 in
the UK by Boxtree, an imprint of Pan Macmillan.

Printed and bound in the United States of America.
VP 10 9 8 7 6 5 4 3 2 1

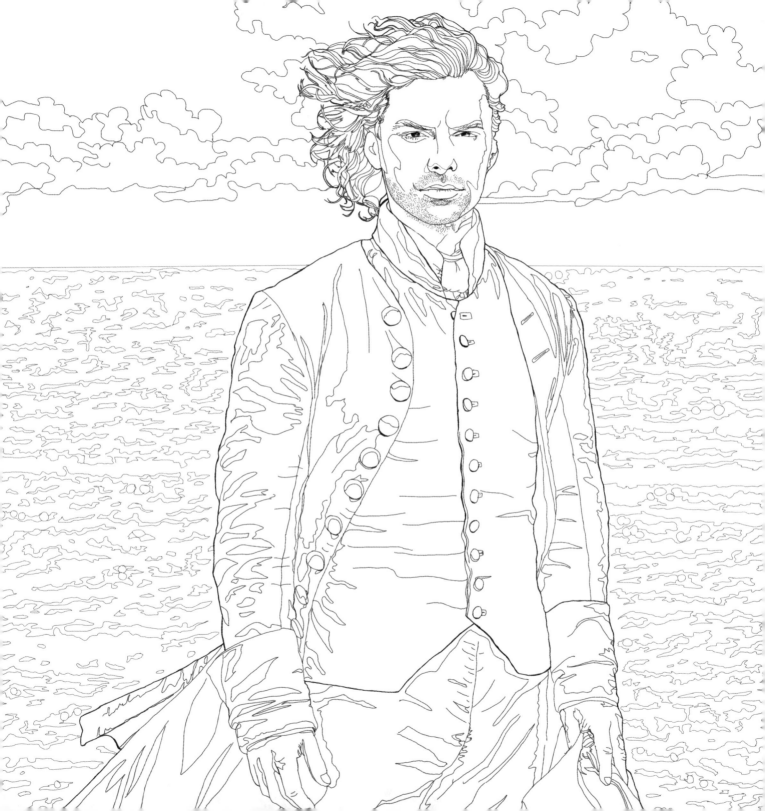

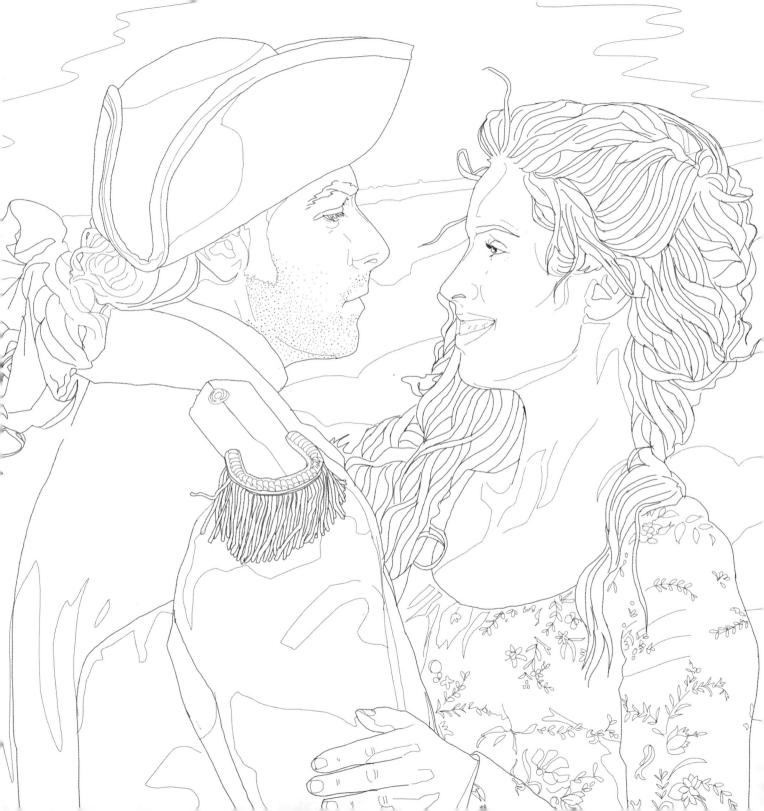

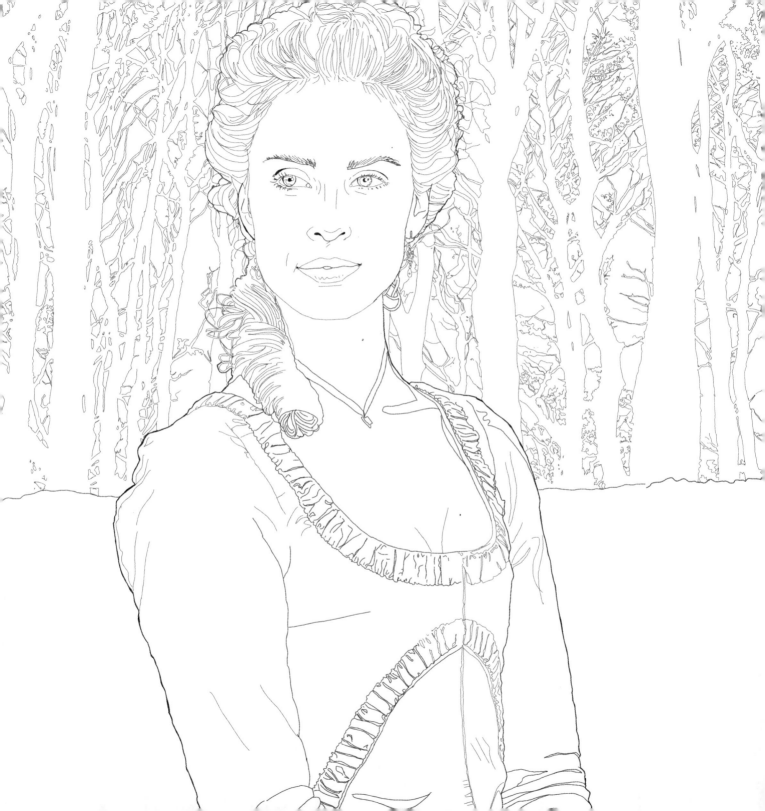

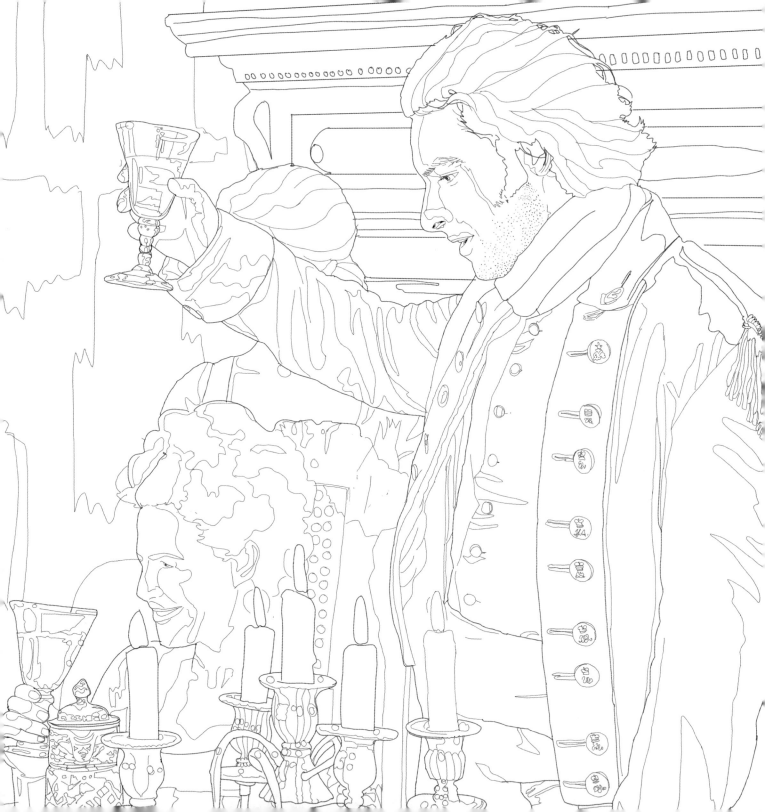

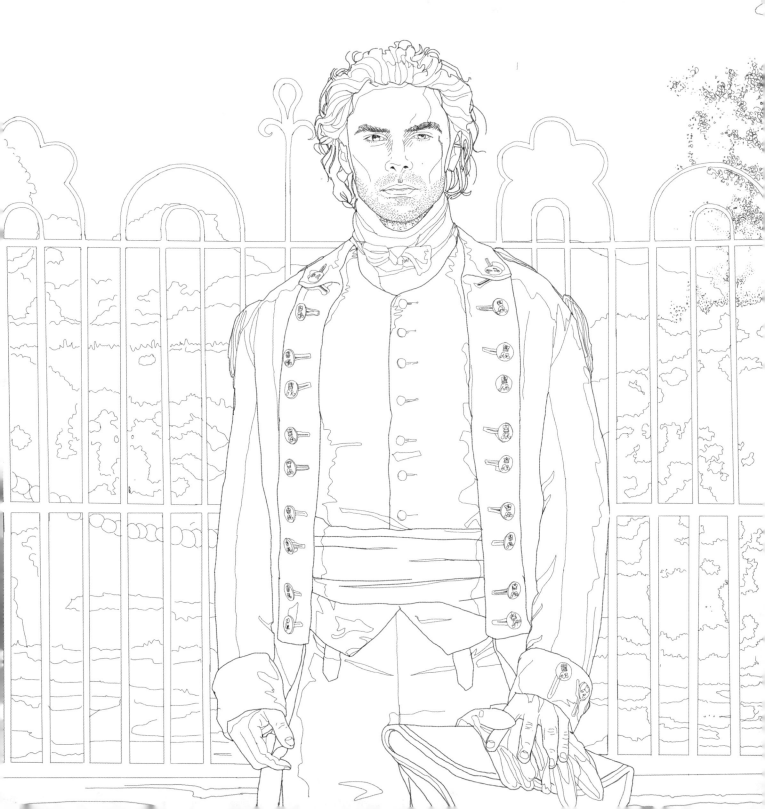

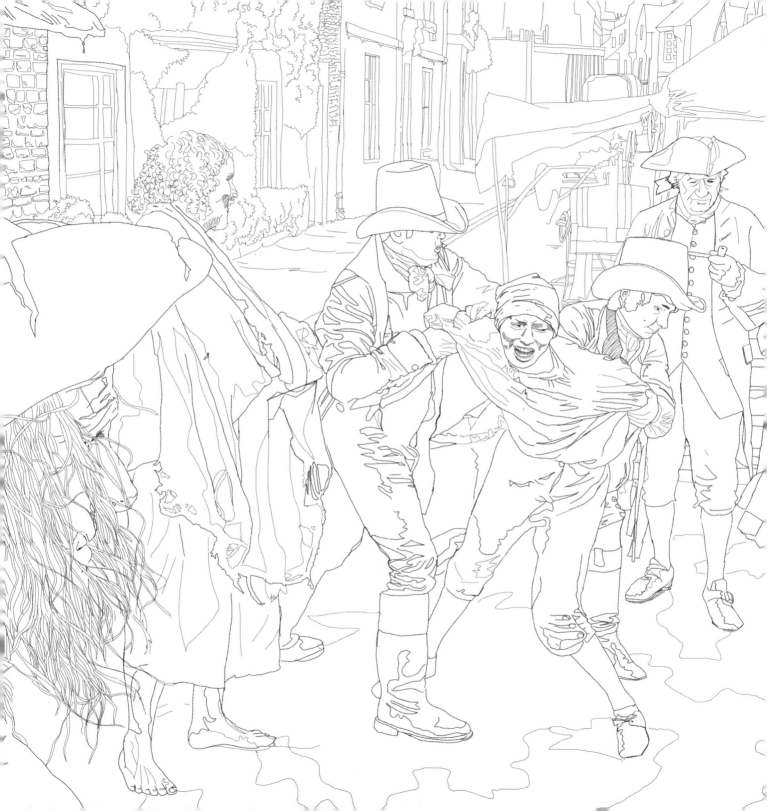

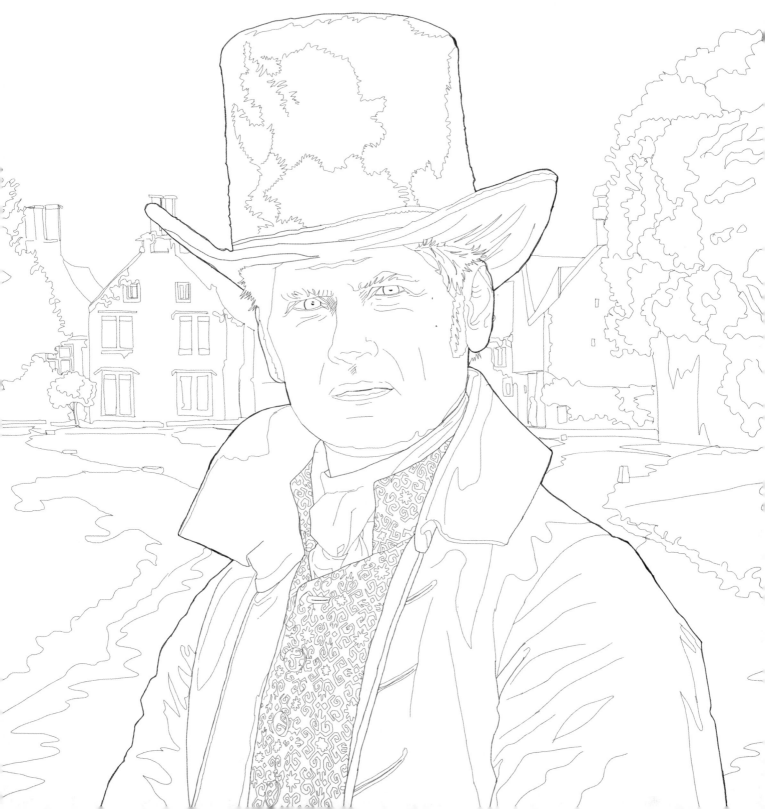

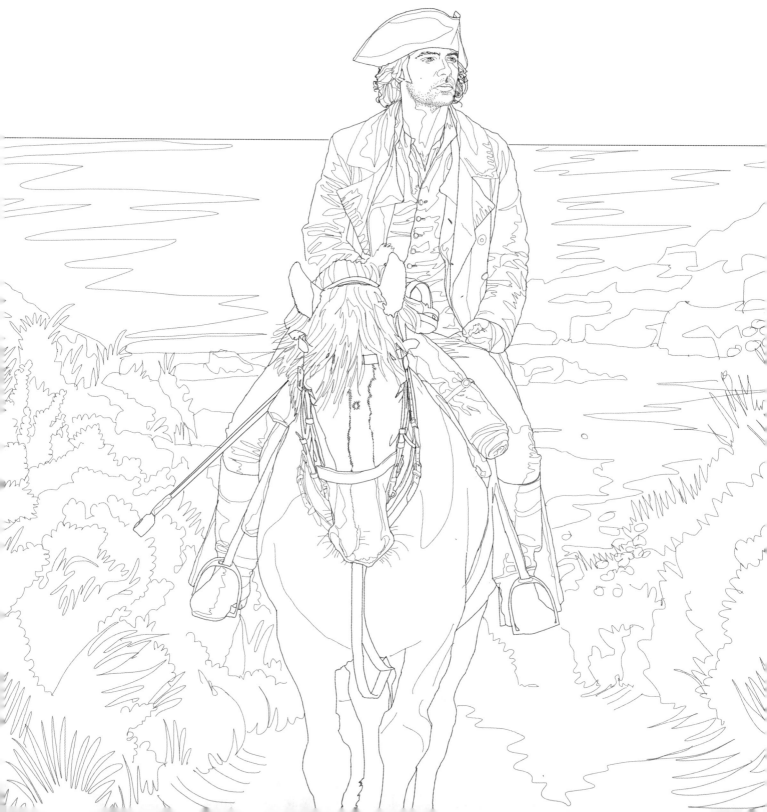

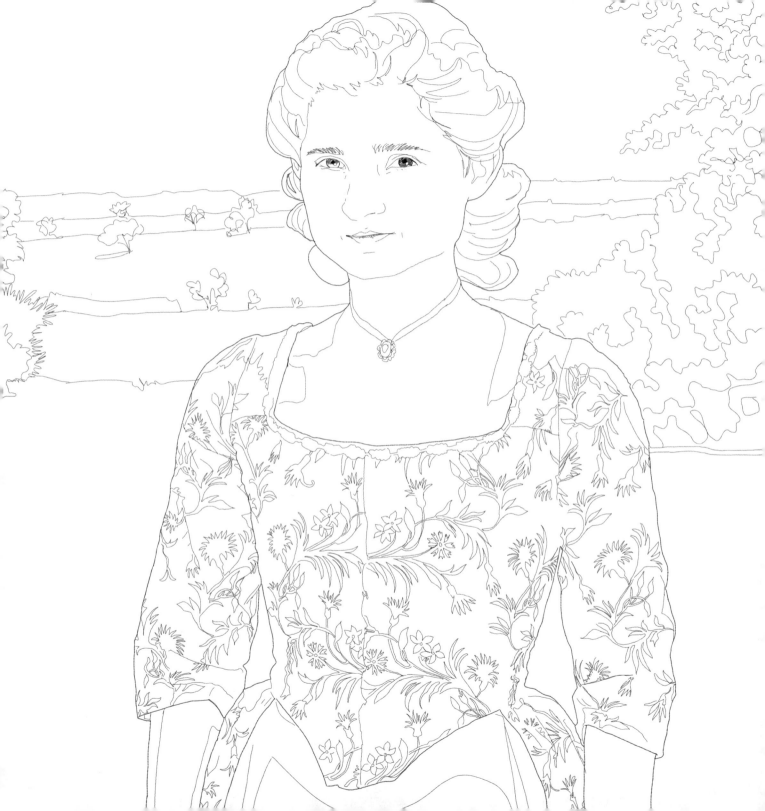

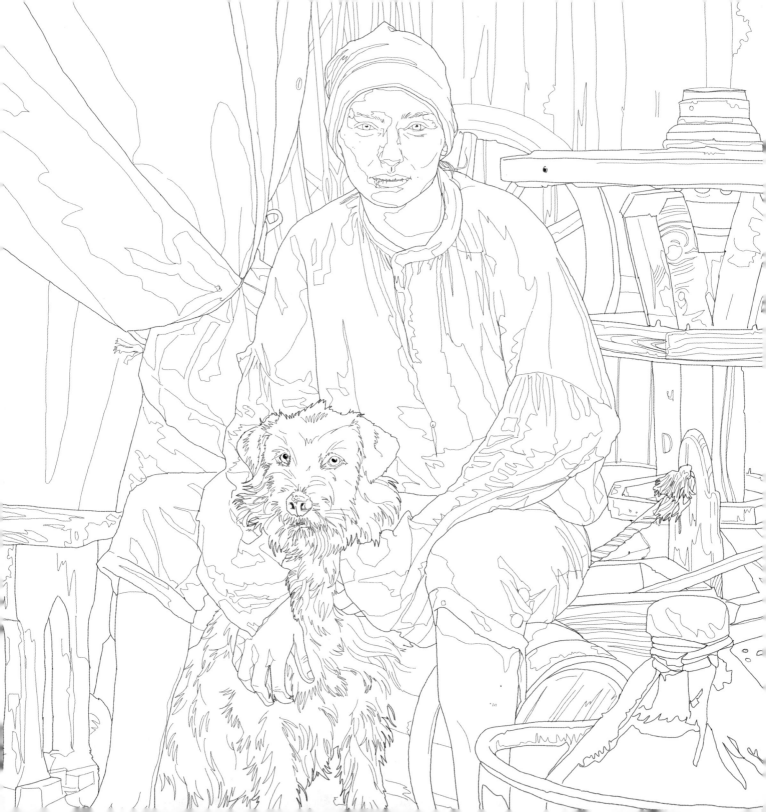

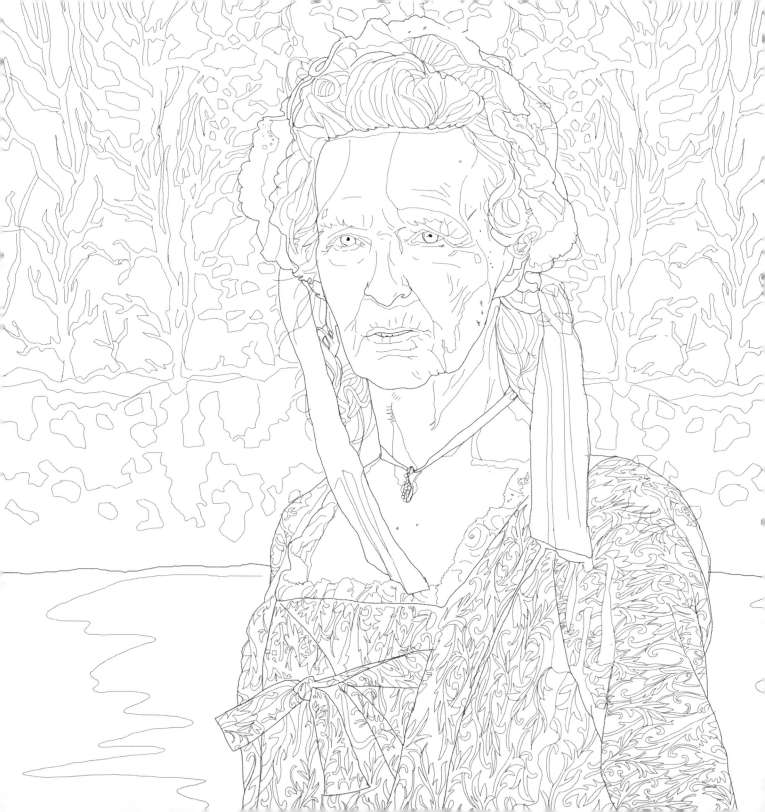

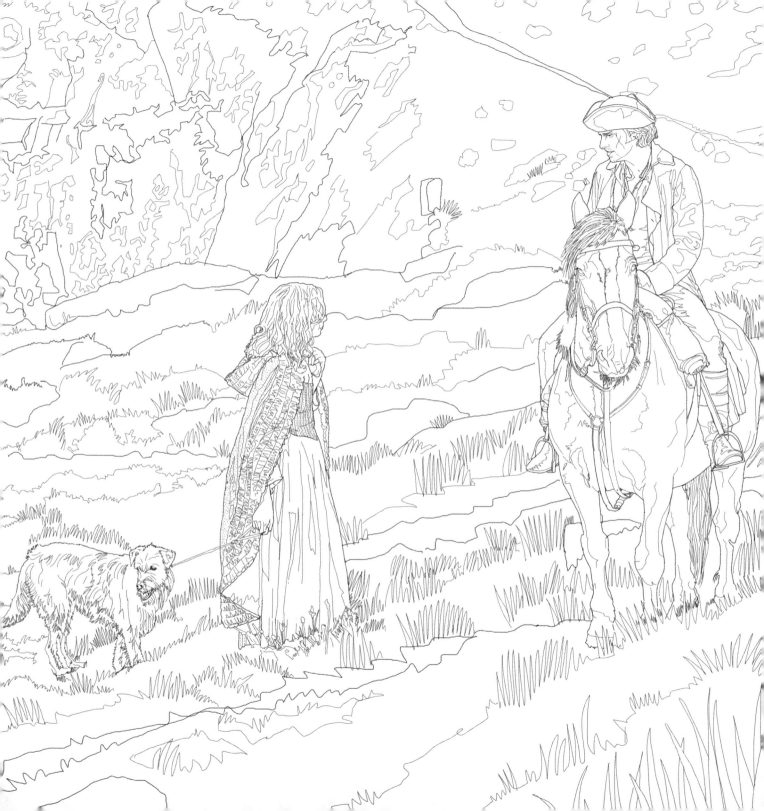

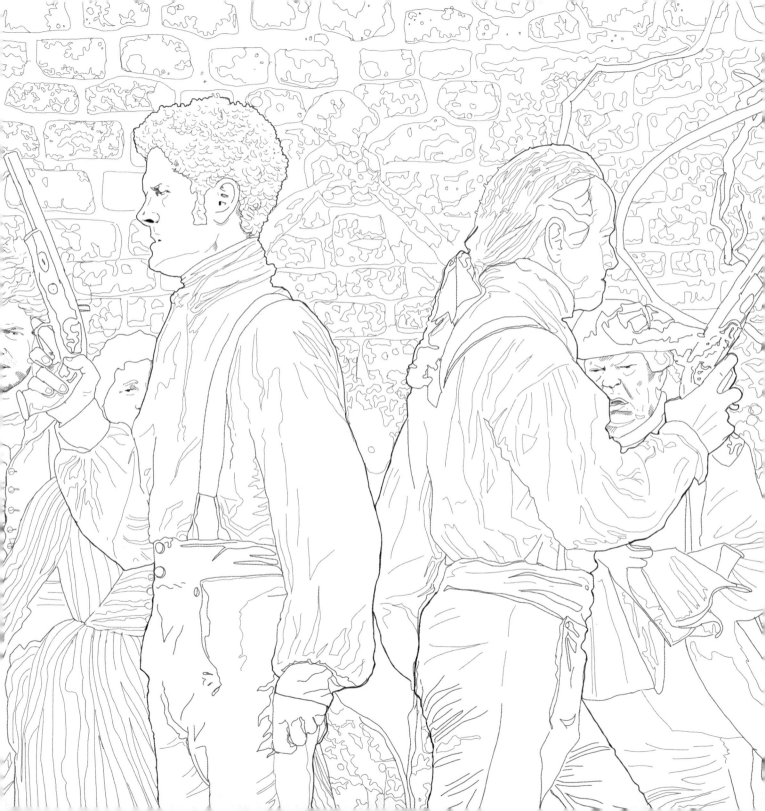

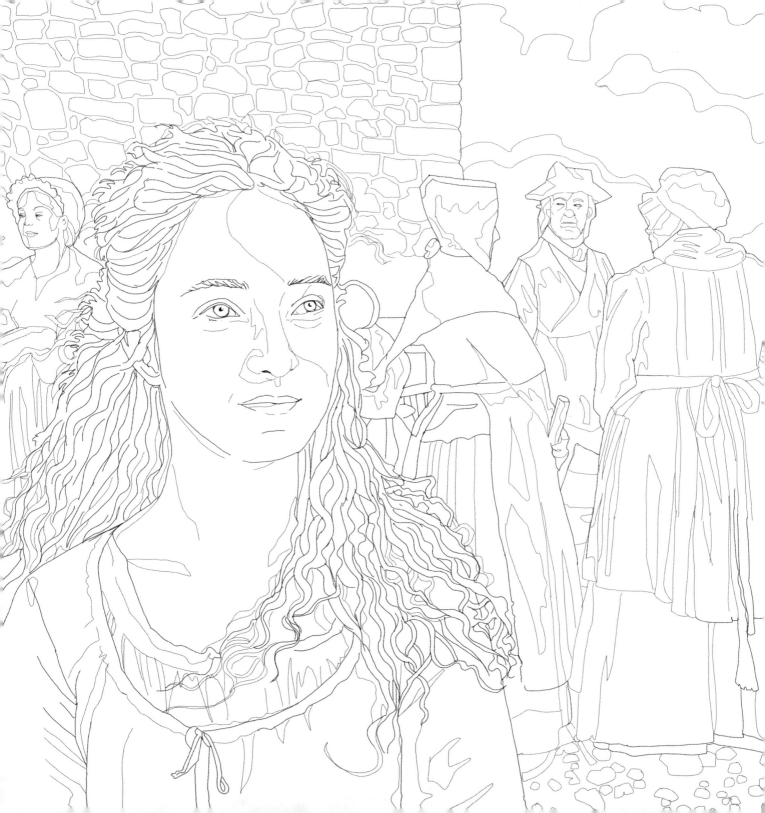

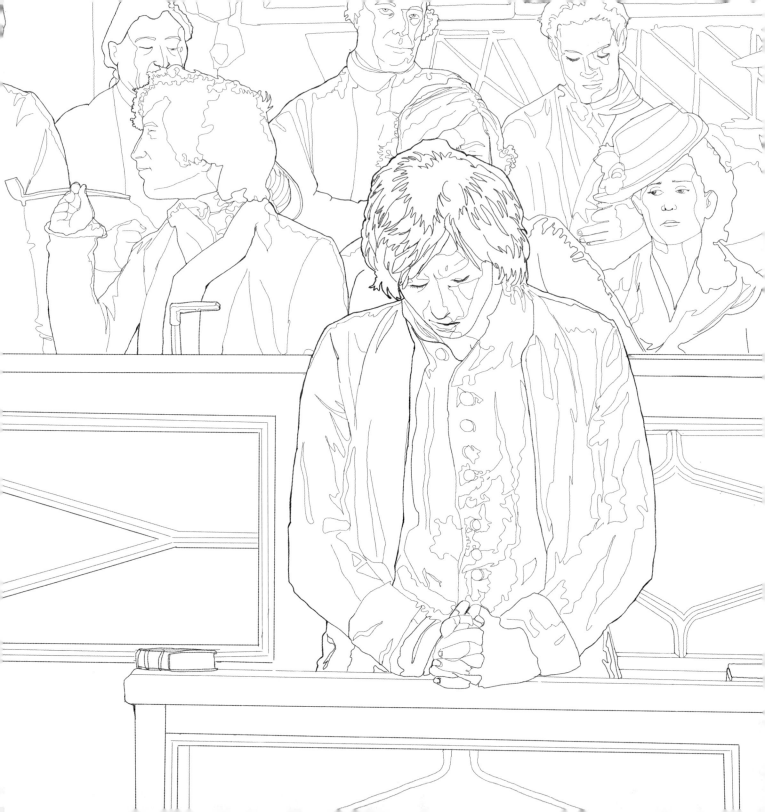

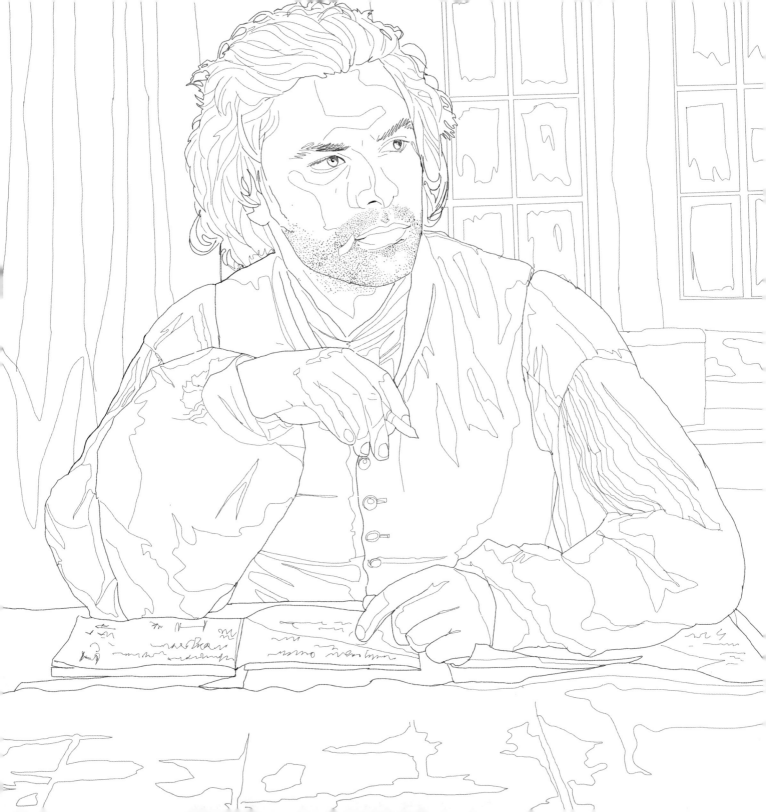

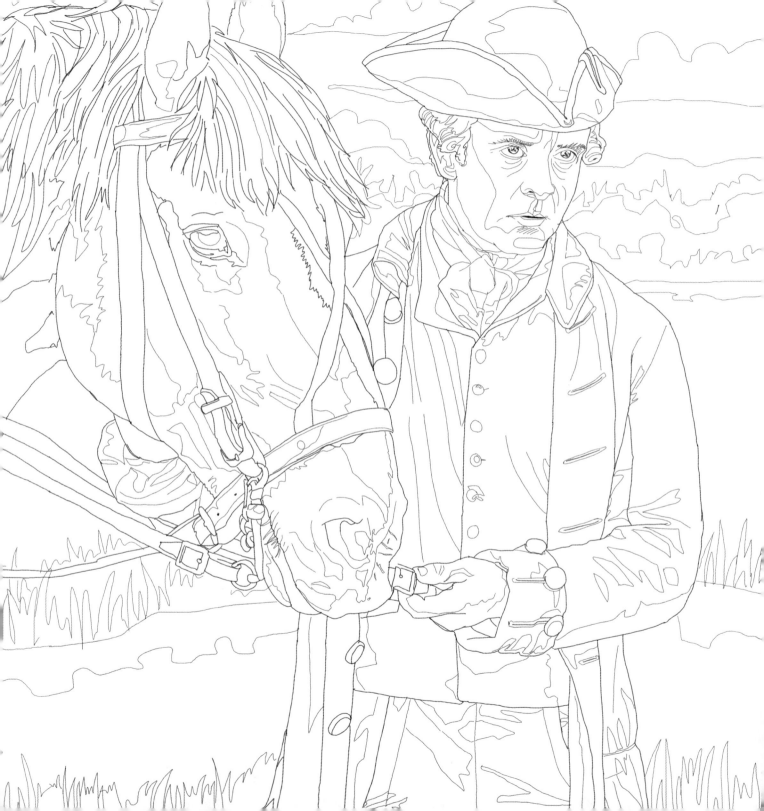

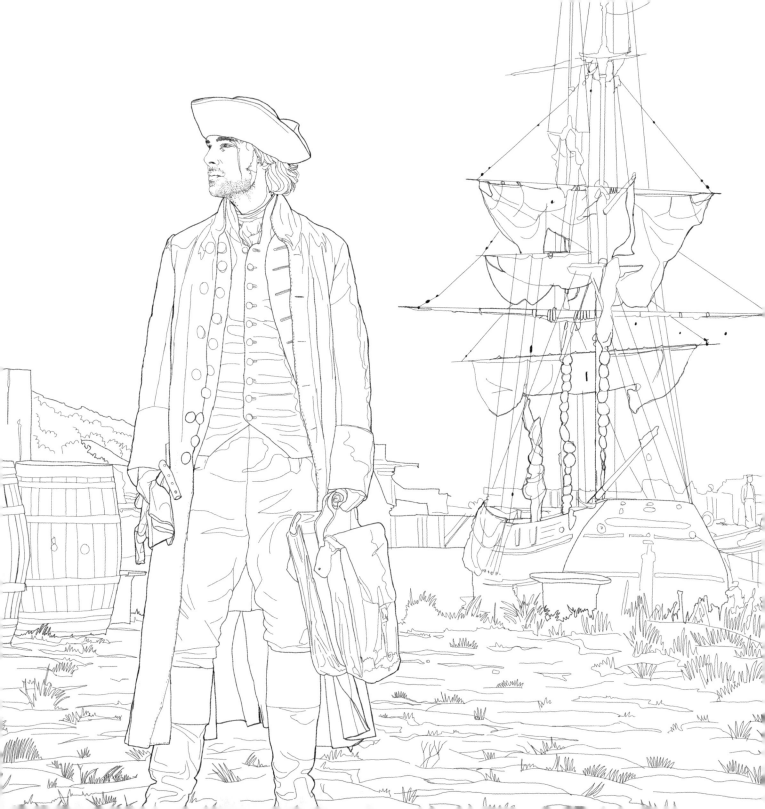

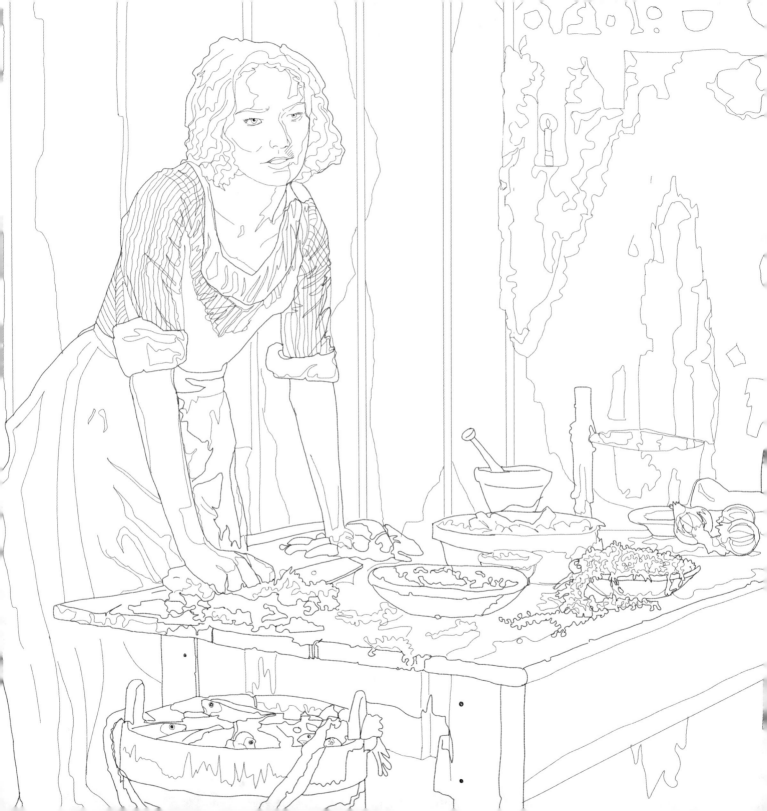

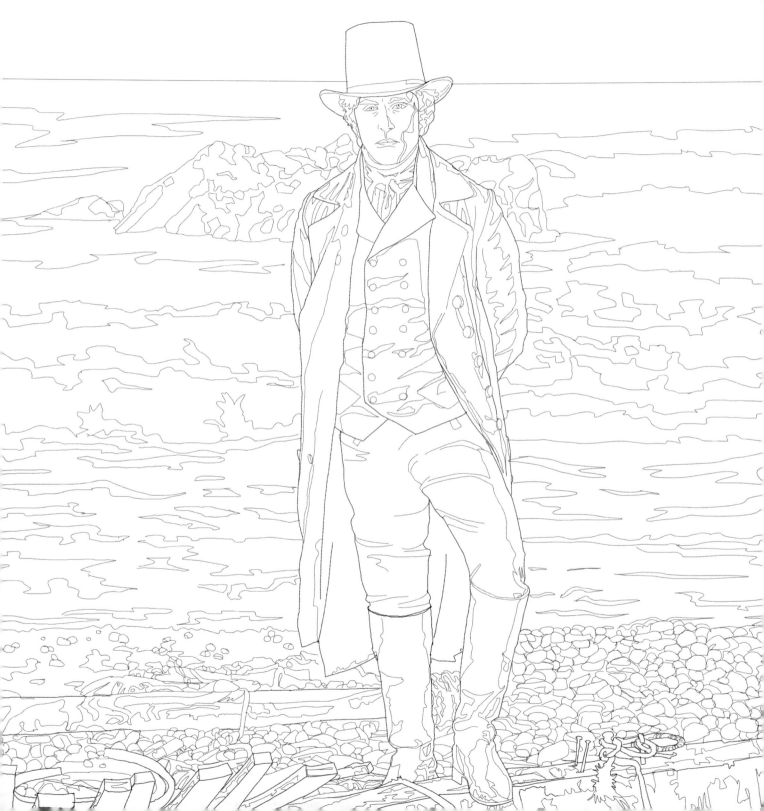

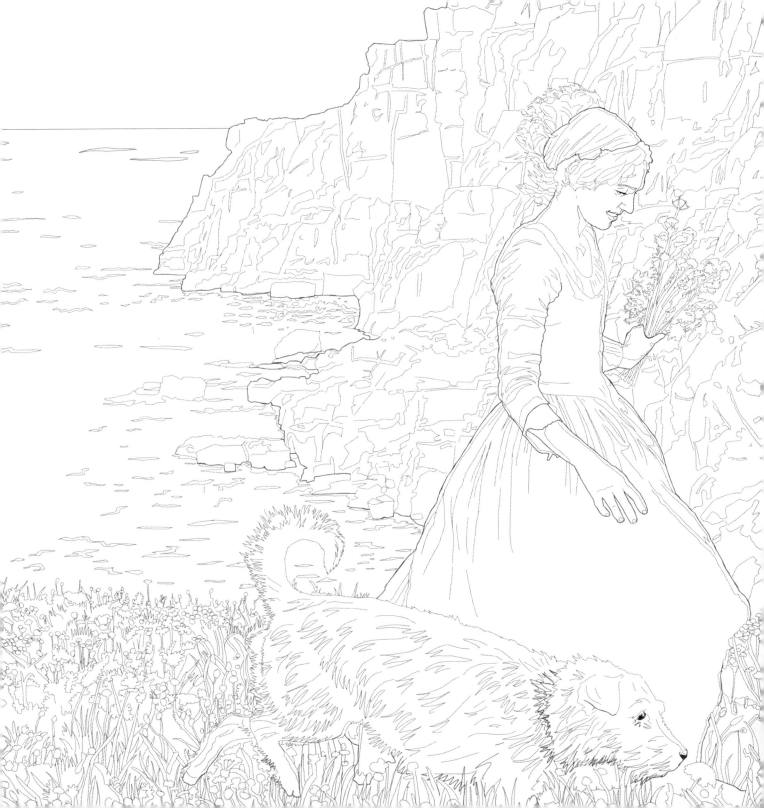

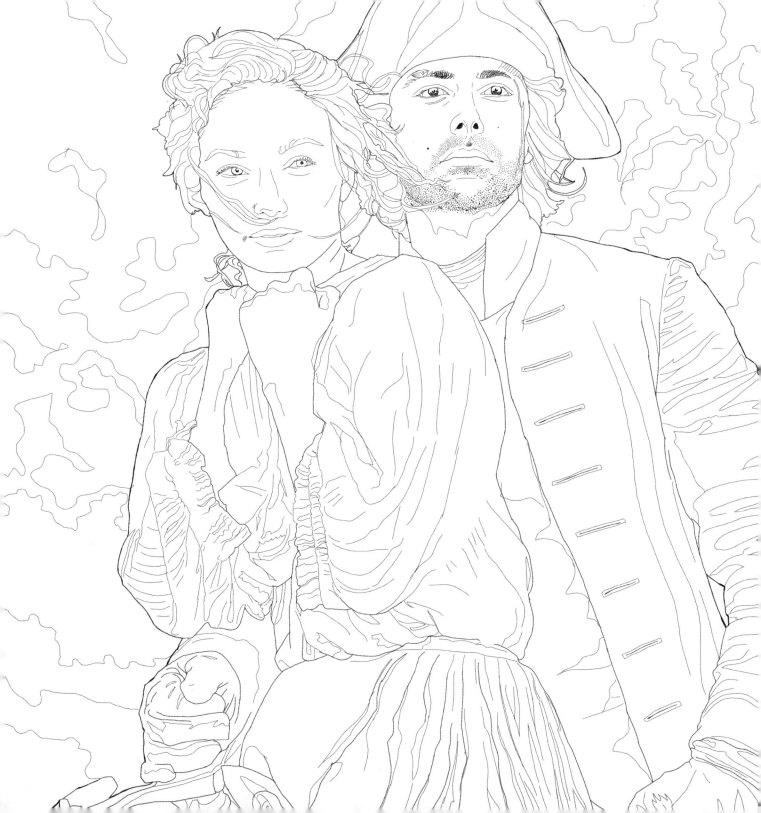

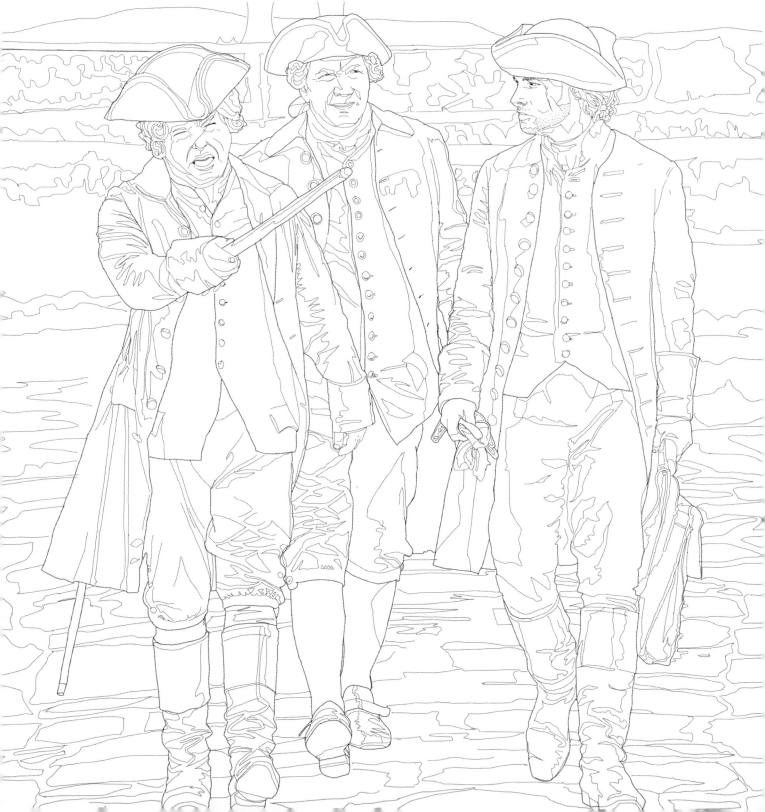

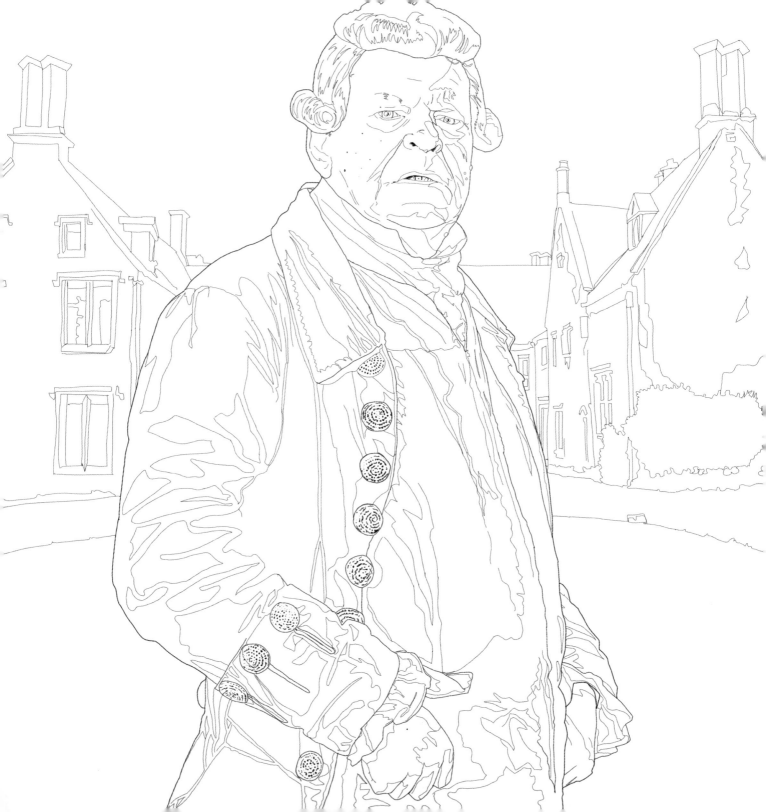

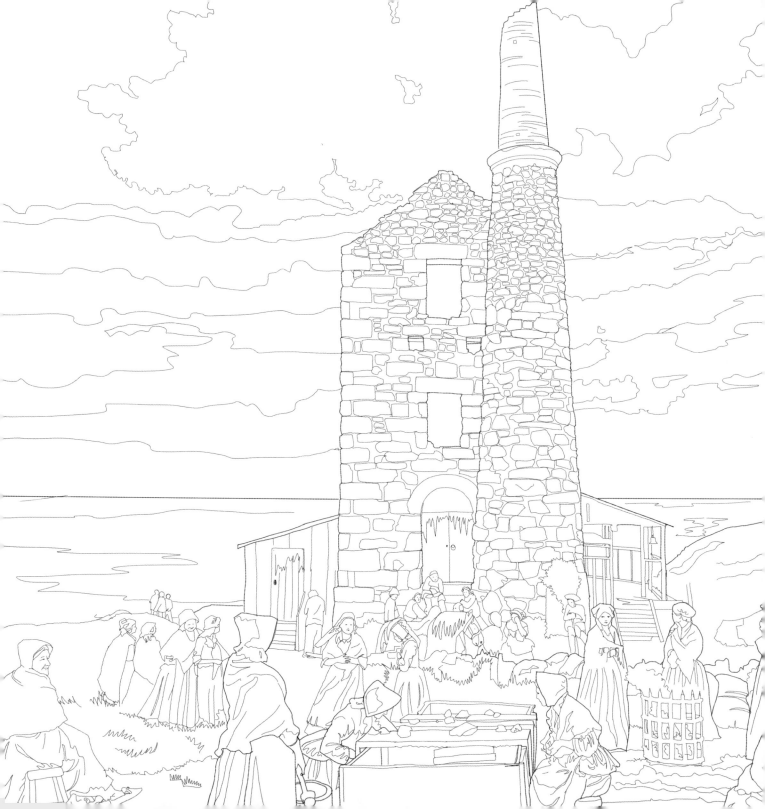

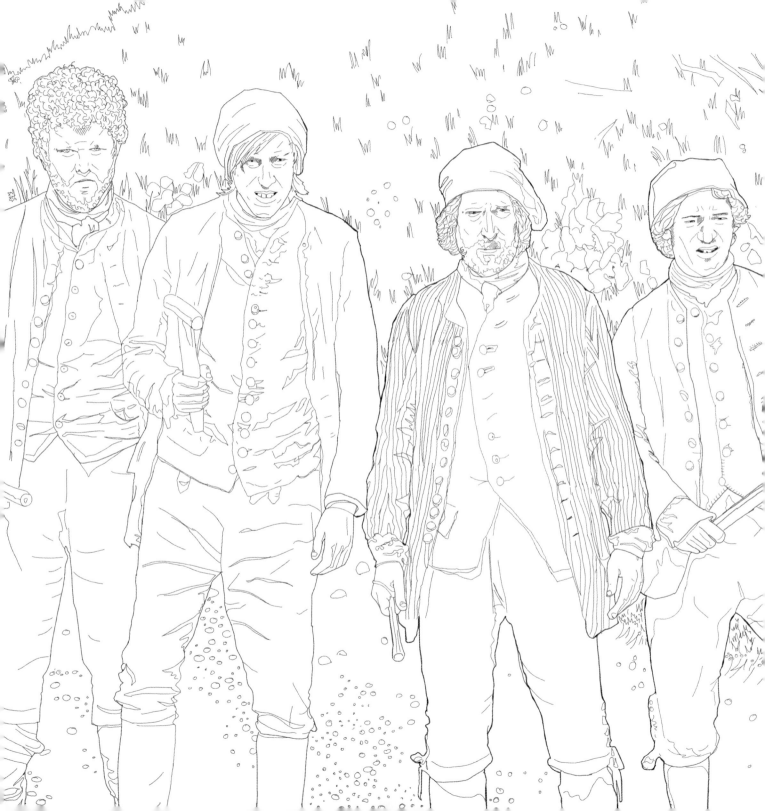

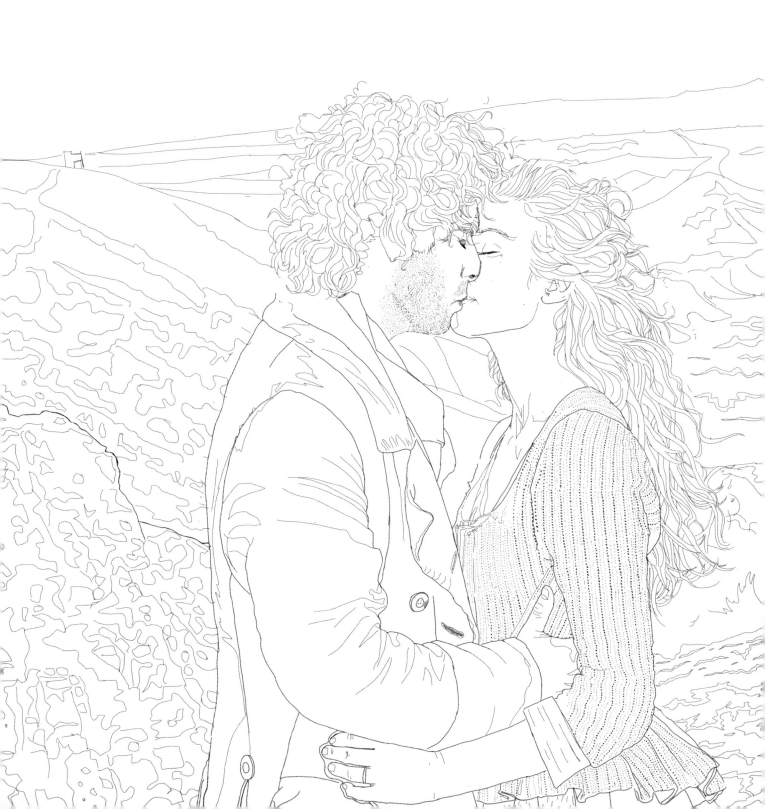

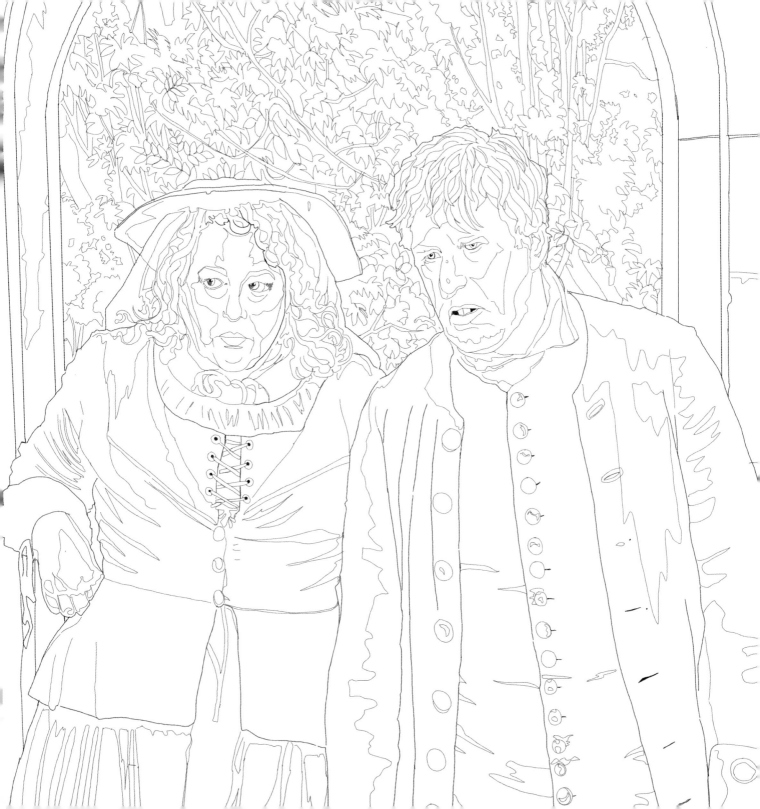

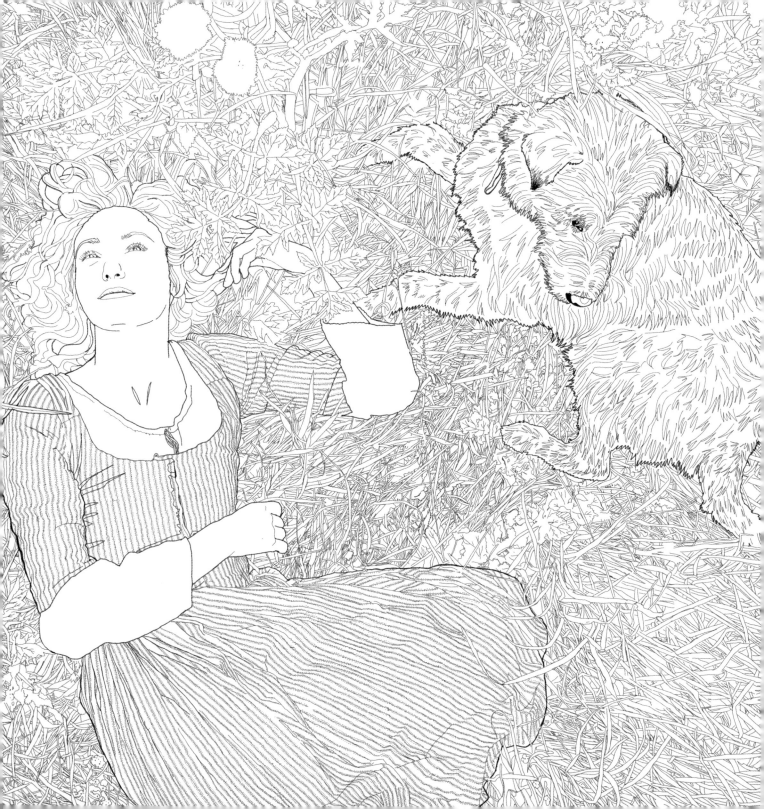

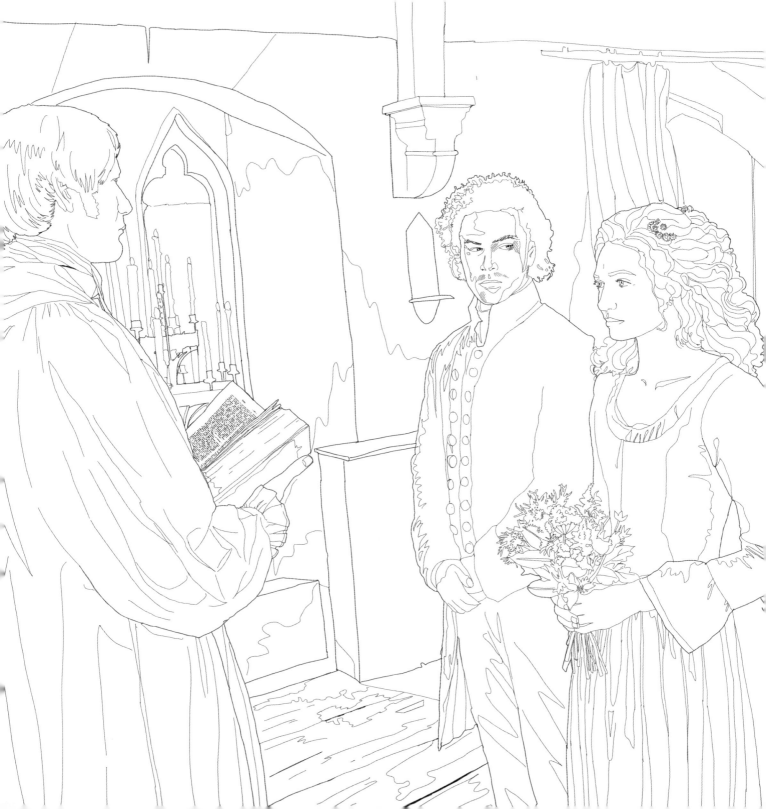

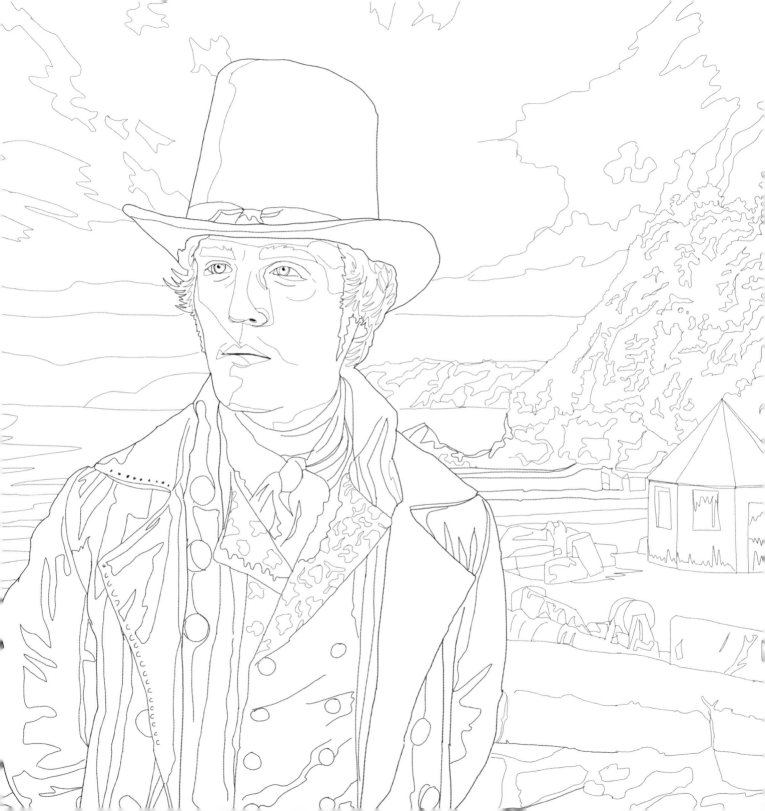

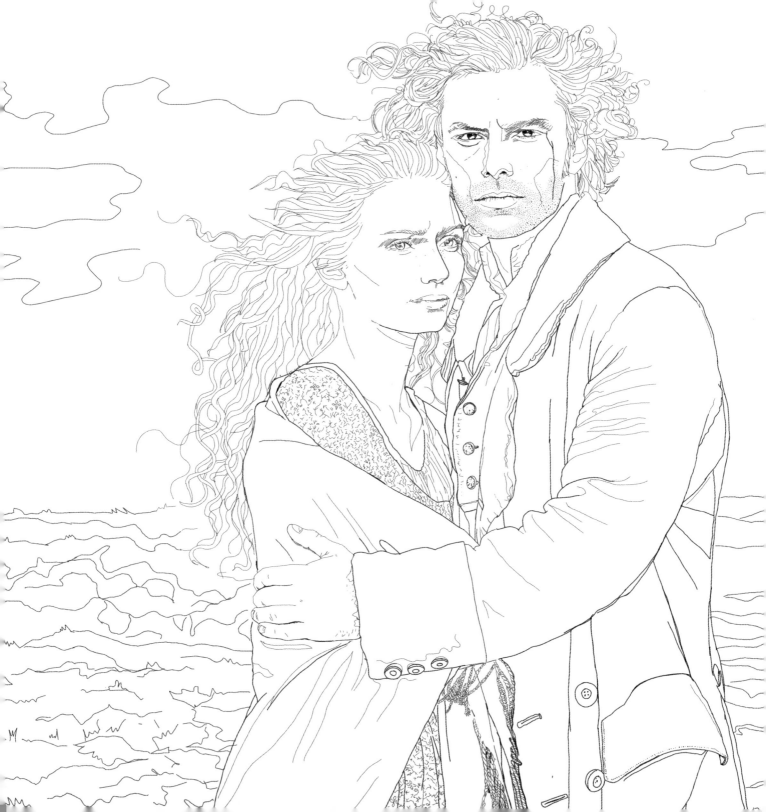

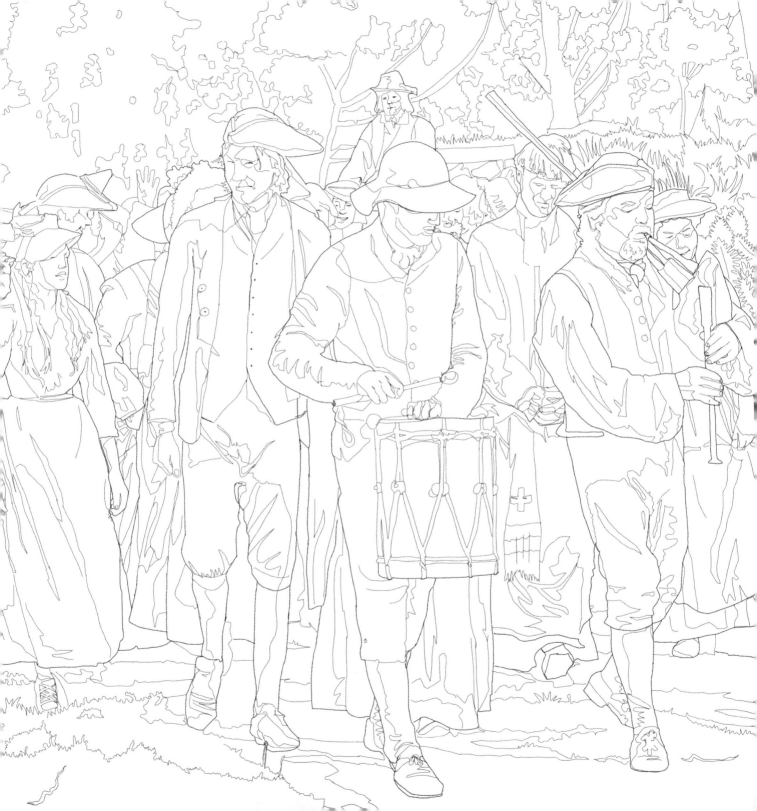

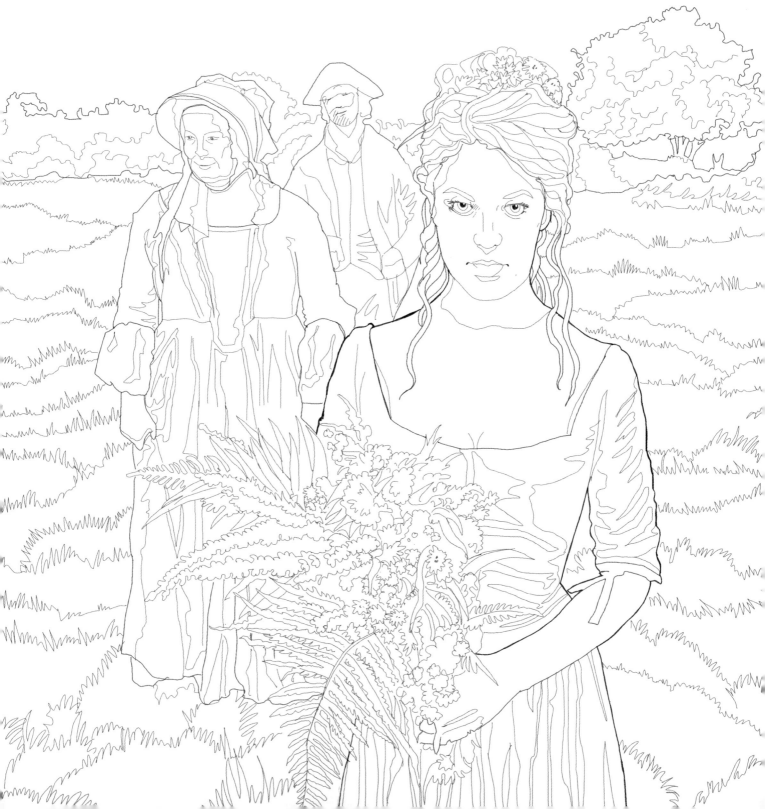

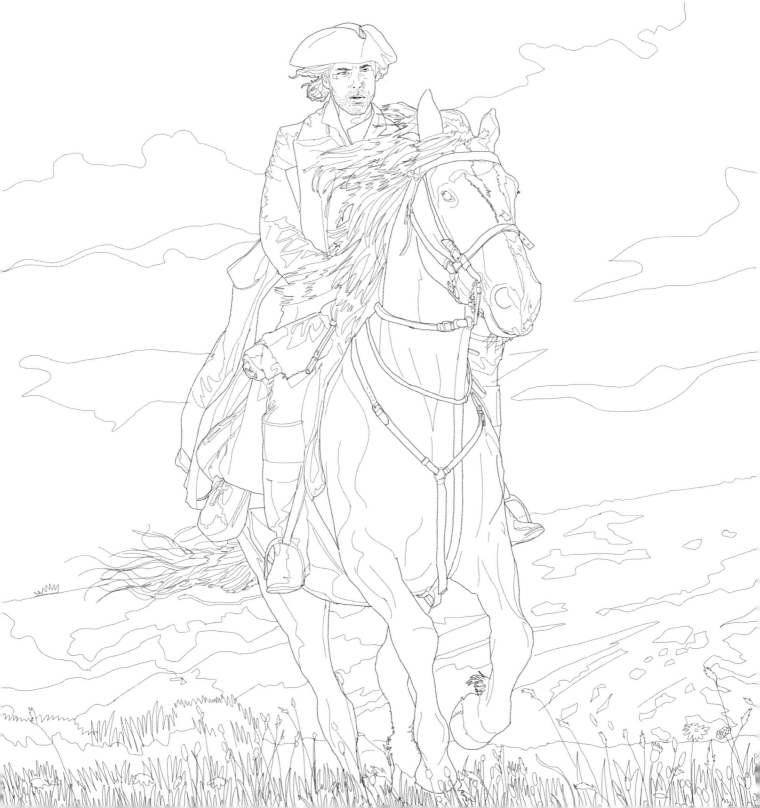

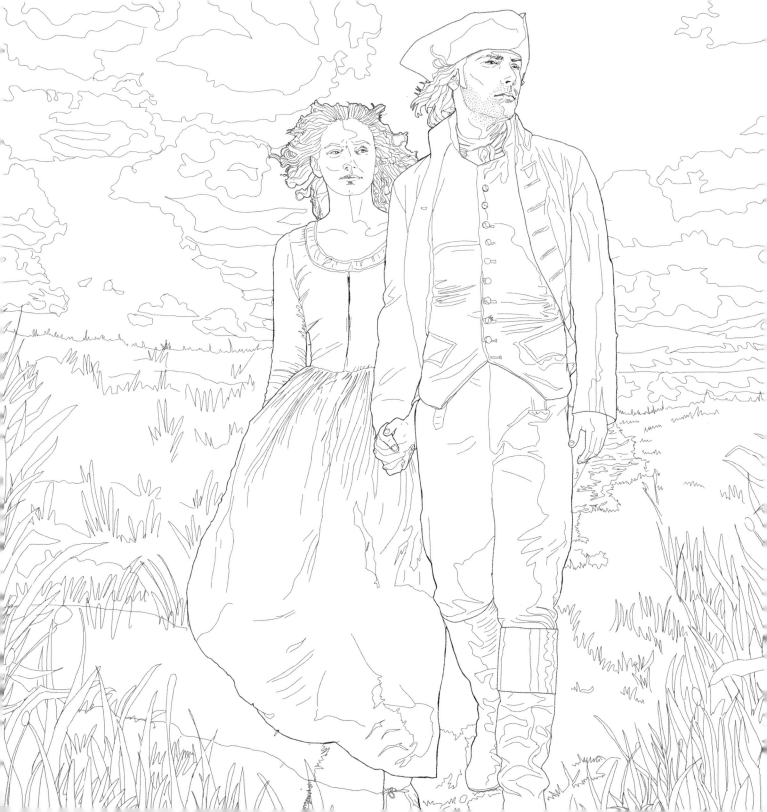

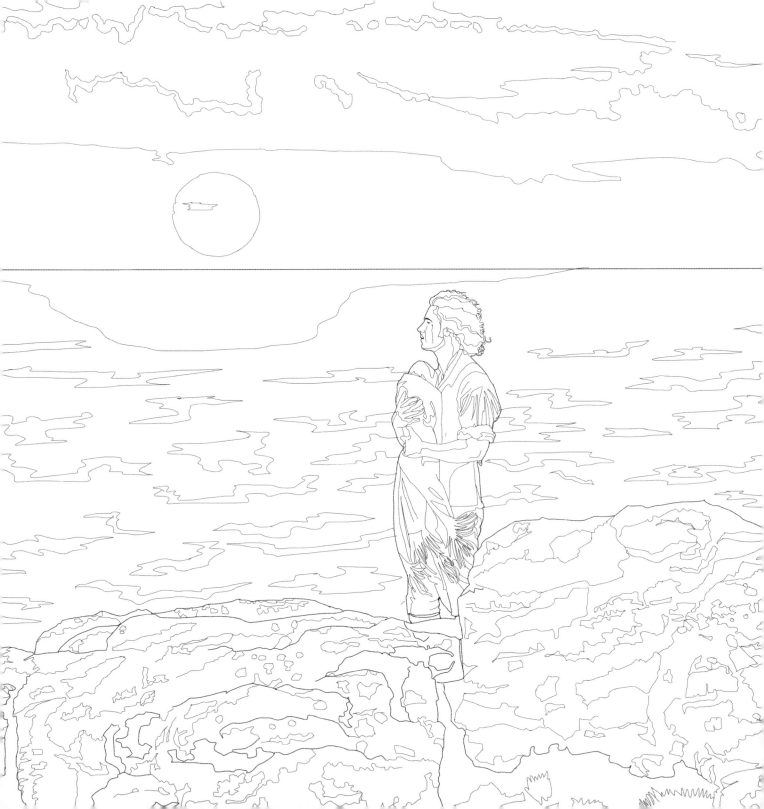

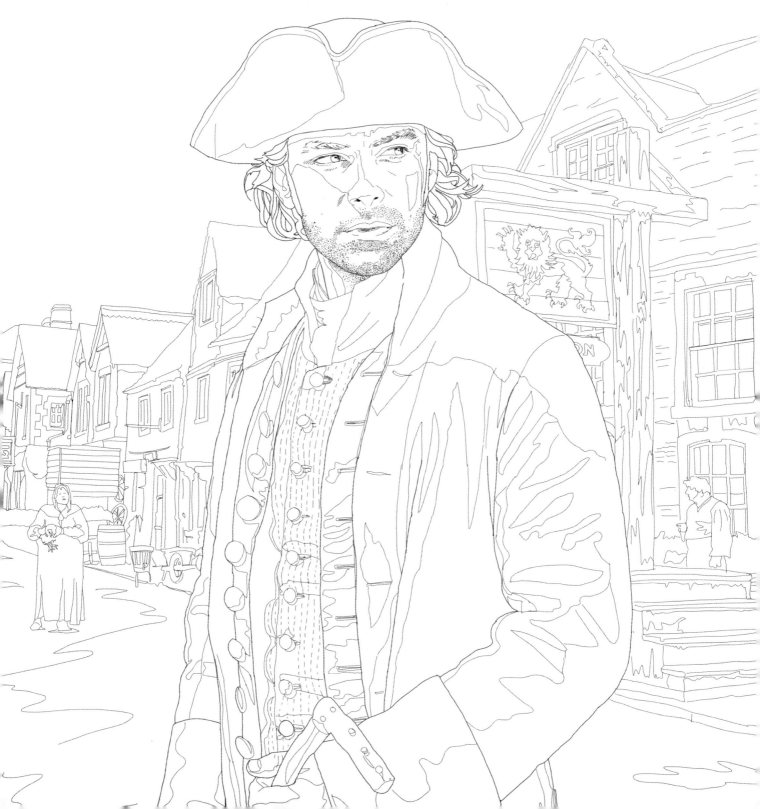

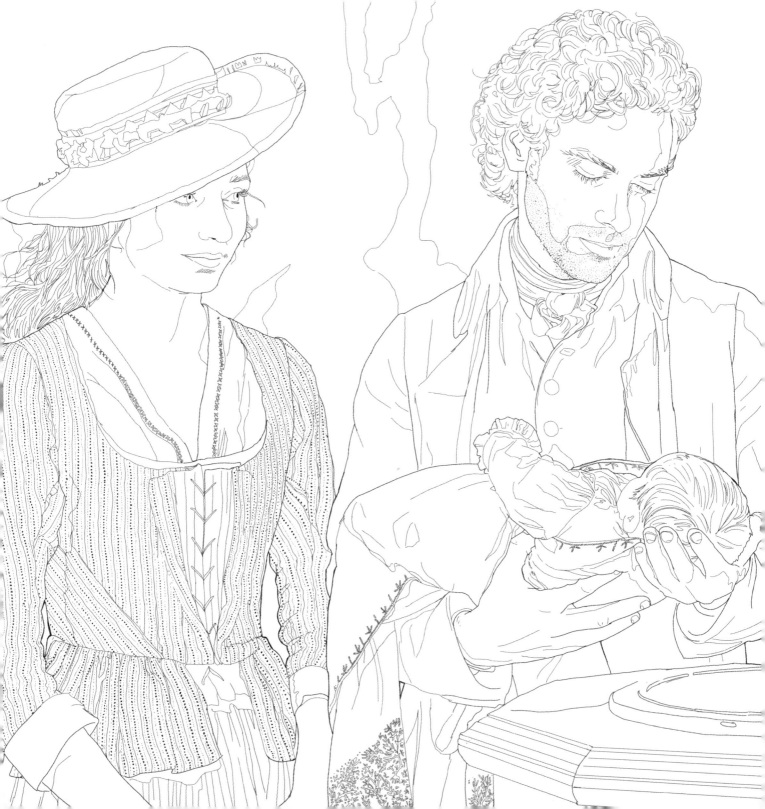

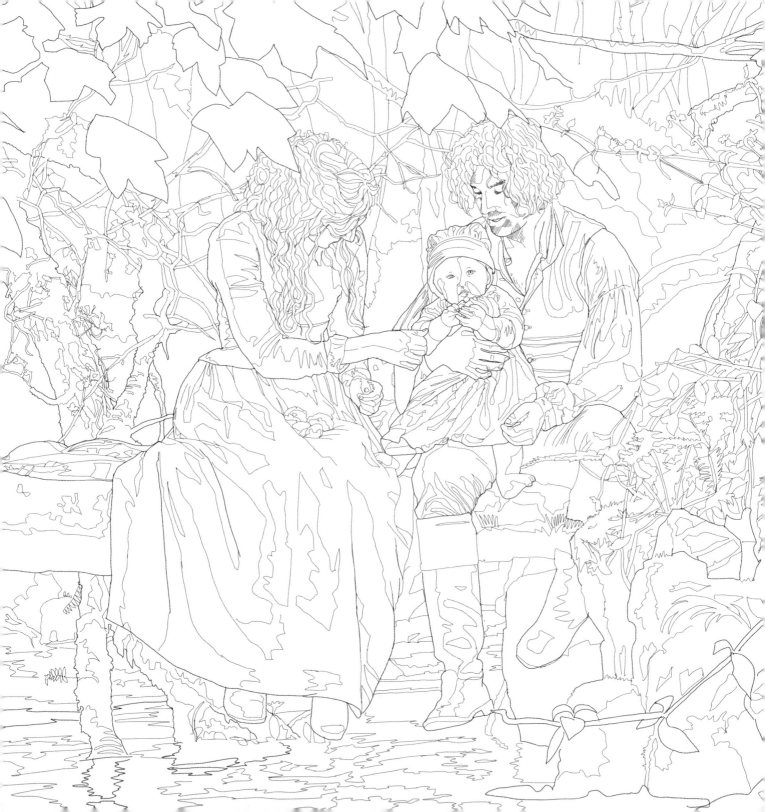

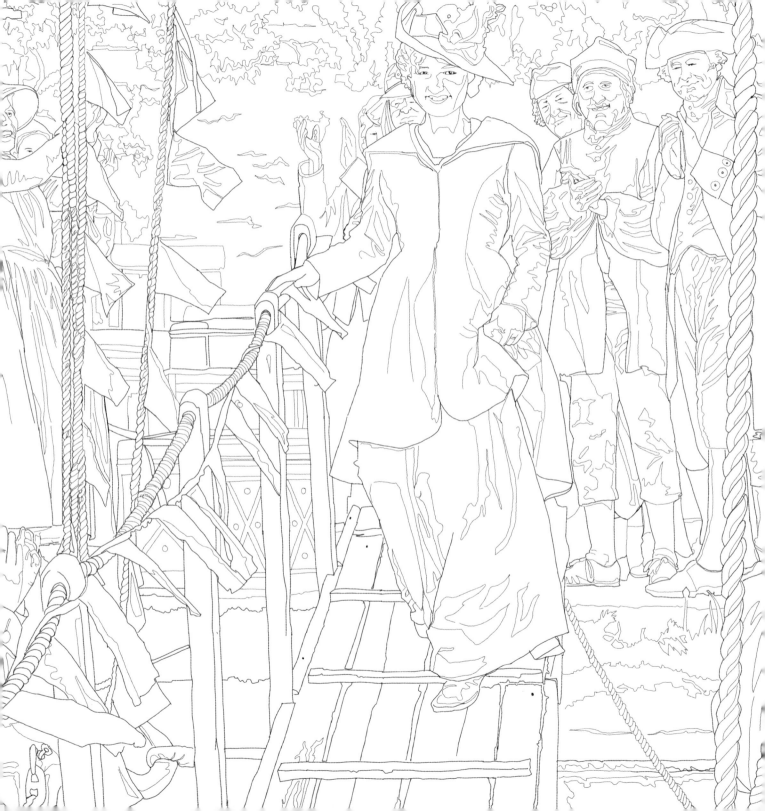

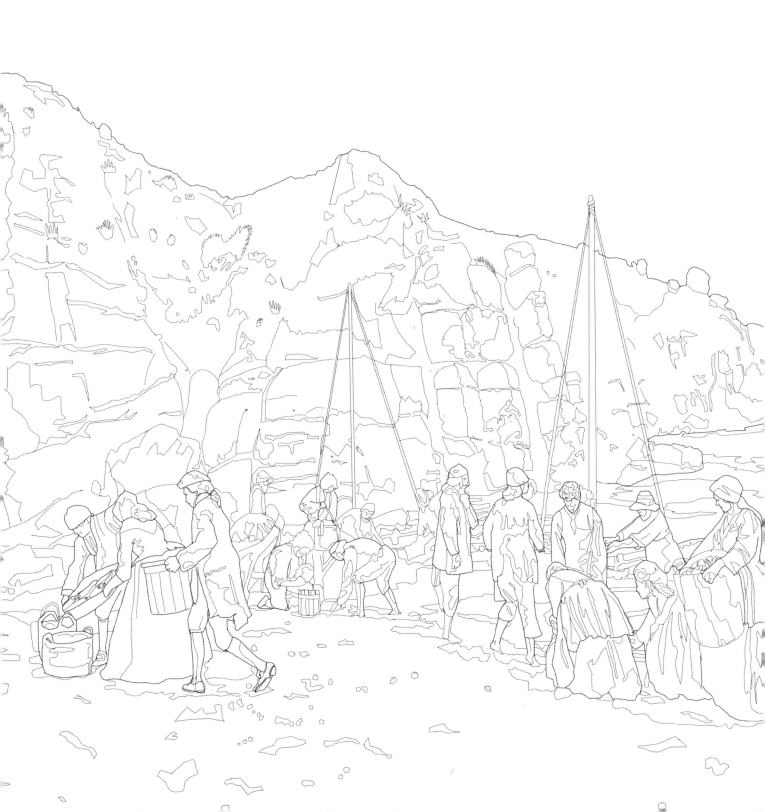

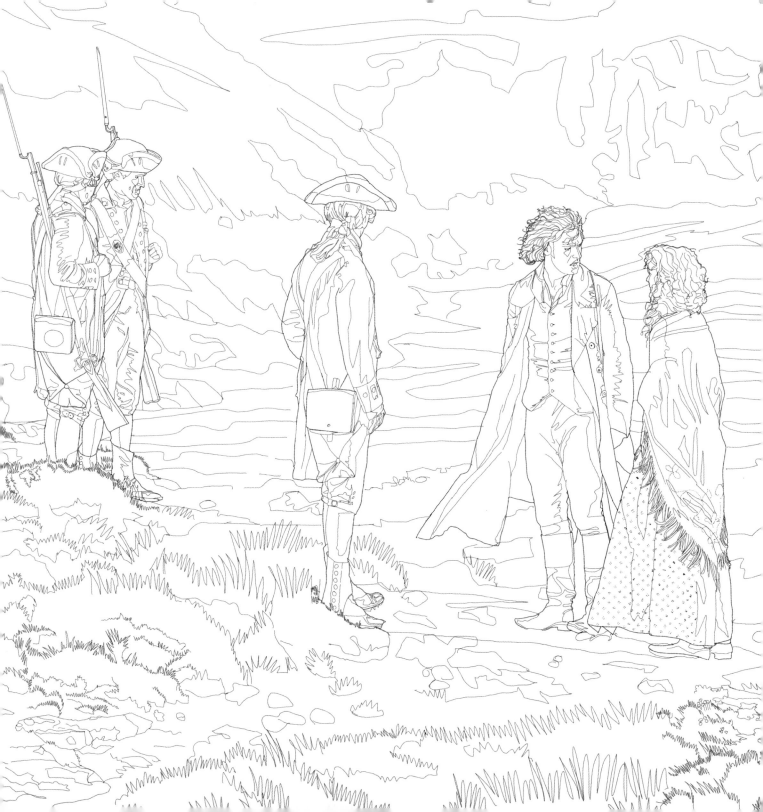

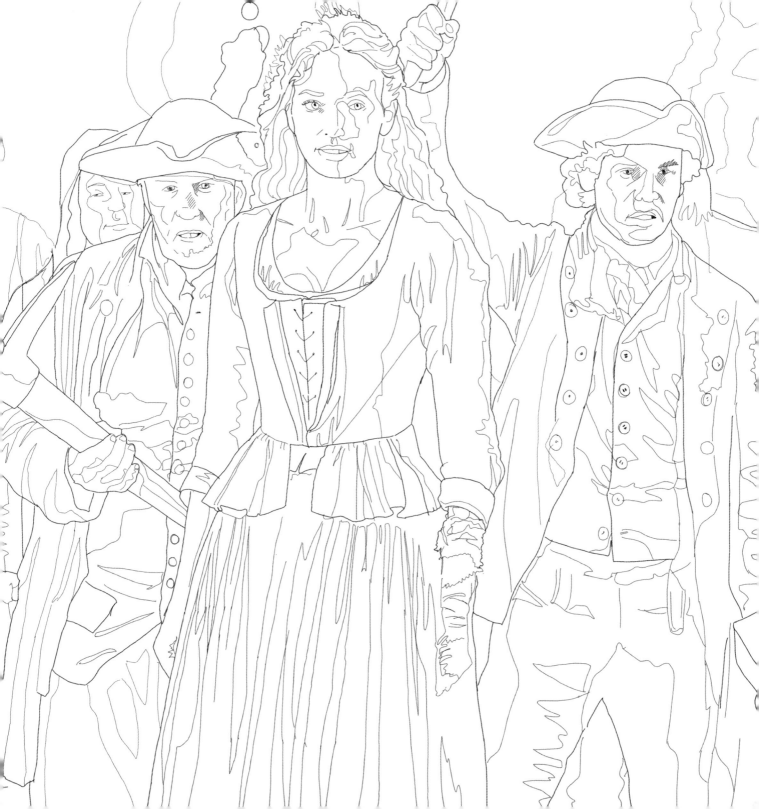

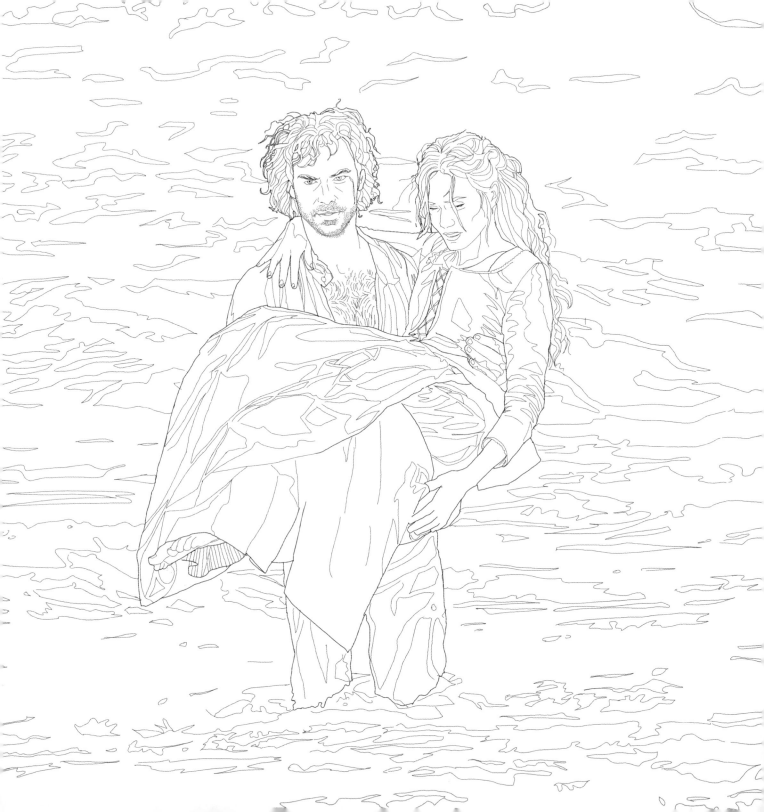

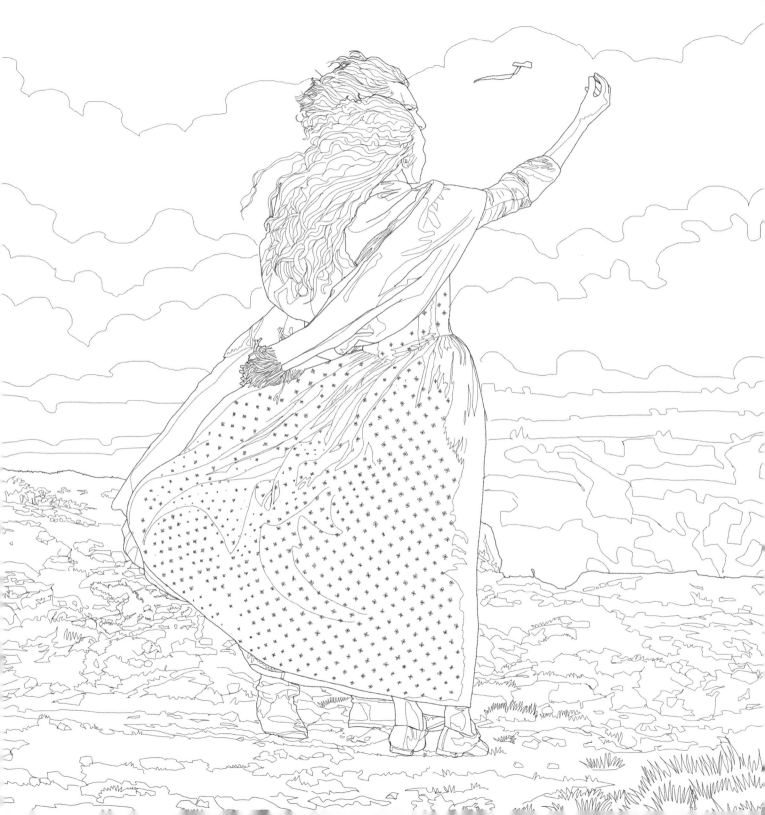